Nocturne

Poems of Love,
Distance,
and the Night,
a callous and disinterested lover

"I was not yet in love, yet I loved to love…I sought what I might love, in love with loving."   --Augustine of Hippo

Preface to the First Print Edition

As I mentioned in the first edition, these poems were written from about 1985 to 1993, during which time I was an officer in the US Navy. This was a time of rapid and frequent change for me in many ways, including geographically, emotionally, professionally, and romantically. Some of these are based on actual events; others are fiction designed to capture the spirit of the moment.

I have arranged these not in chronological order, but in an order that tells what I perceive as the story of my spiritual and emotional development during those years.

To help the narrative flow, I have eliminated the titles of many poems and left only a few, which are important to the understanding of the poem.

In this second edition, I have included poems, published or unpublished, that were left out of the first for various reasons, the primary one being they were simply lost or forgotten. Another reason, for one at least, is because it alluded to an intimate moment, and being naturally somewhat shy and reserved, I felt embarrassed at publishing it initially. I am still a little embarrassed, but I am getting over it and this poem (or two) does support the character development of the unnamed narrator and gives a more refined feel for the emotional environment of the overall story.

I have woven these additional poems into the text to help support the narrative instead of including them as a second part, which would seem out of place, out of the chronological flow, and simply awkward.

Because the cost of a print edition with color photos would be prohibitively expensive, I have left out the photos in the Kindle edition. Maybe one day I will be able to produce a coffee table version of *Nocturne* and include all the photos I would like and make them as big as I like.

I would love to leave something like that behind, a work of beauty visually, emotionally, and intellectually, as part of my literary and spiritual legacy.

In any case, I hope you enjoy this humble effort as it currently stands.

There are other poems that remain from this time, but they are lost somewhere among my scattered possessions at my parents' estate. They are my earliest poems from when I lived on Whidbey Island from 1985-1988, the time period in which many of those included here originated. They are also perhaps the most poignant for me in many ways. I look for them when I have the rare chance. If I can ever find them, I shall include them in a future edition.

Phil Slattery
Gillett, Arkansas
August 8, 2020

Introduction

Come with me, my love
and I will show you
nights of love
full of life and laughter
as empty as an empty
bottle rattling down a cobblestone
street blown by a chill
wind

Come with me, my love
and I will show you
nights of love
full of lust and passion
as lonely as a lonely
man pacing off a deserted street
under the brisk October moon
its cold light muted
in the mists

As the fog embraces you
like a one-night stand in a town
of dying dreams where
hopes lie scattered on the barroom floor
with cigarette butts and the dust
of endless roads

Bring me to that ultimate pleasure
in your all-consuming eyes.
Let us become one
and share the horrors of this
world
as only
lovers can.

Let us go beyond the boundaries of love
into realms uncharted
into areas forbidden

Reserved only for the animals
and the lowliest of the low

Let us explore
and grasp into each other's soul
reaching into the very heart of each other's being

We are beyond the perversions and twisted fantasies of
this morbid little world.

Let us step beyond
where no one dares tread
let us claw our way into each other's essence
becoming more than one in our revelry
becoming lovers

You turn your eyes, smiling
as we make love
your smooth brown shoulders
peer from under my worn flannel shirt
not buttoned, draping loosely

In the dark I can barely see the slight dark curves
perfect breasts peeping from behind pockets
darker spots smooth to tongue tip
inane shyness
must wear a shirt
embarrassed to let me see
have to turn as she undresses
slips between the sheets

Tender woman
innocence, laughter, and smile
strength of soul forged in sorrow, woman
needle in cotton

Raven black hair
Eyes dark and warm as a summer night
She hovers between my heart and my mind

Sunlight come wake me from a gentle sleep
Shine golden and warm upon my face
As I softly awake to the brightness of the new day
And wipe the memories of last night's love
From these sleepy eyes
But never from my heart.

I would
Like to take this
Opportunity to
Very briefly
Explain to
You why I
Often seemed lost
Until now.

I love you as I love the dawn
      and the glowing beauty it brings

I love you as I love the early morn'
      and the quiet peace it brings to my soul

I love you as I love the afternoon
      and the golden warmth it shines upon me

I love you as I love the evening
      and the rest it grants to my weary body

I love you as I love the sunset
      red as your lips
      darkening breeze gentle as your
      breath upon my cheek

I love you as I love the night
      dark and sparkling as your eyes
      full of mystery and passion
      ever leading back
      to the dawn

I can read you like a book
I can see the anger beneath those furrowed brows
I can the passion repressed
      in every slow silky movement
I can see every plotting manipulative gleam
      in those darkest of eyes
I can see the tender sorrow
      in that quietly bowed head
I can see the greatest mercy
      in that most wicked of smiles
I can see the purest love
      in the most intense anger
Because of all these
I love you all the more intensely

Two hands

    Playing a guitar

One
    Sets the chords

One
    Gives life to the strings

Together
    Conceiving a magic
    Of which neither is capable

alone

I imagine myself on a plain awash in twilight
the last golden glow upon my face and chest
a cool, relentless, overpowering flow
pressing passionately against my body,
running headlong through my hair, filling my ears,
rushing wildly around my sides and thighs,
pulling, tugging crazily at my jeans and shirt
continuously, never ending.

I live for moments such as these
when there is neither hunger nor thirst,
nor past, nor future,
only the eternal, overwhelming moment of the senses.

You are such a moment,
when all other desires are lost in a non-existent past.

Passion in its primordial form
Desire without direction
Release
I am you
Fluttering about your heart
As a moth about a flame

Dream and flow with the colors, my love
Twist yourself into brilliant bonds
     of yellow and red
Explode with fury and entwine
     with the green of your eyes
Become the essence of your soul
Bring into this earth a new creature
Dream becomes reality
Reality becomes dream

sweat
rolls off lovers' bodies
in the still, sultry night

sheets cling to us
tumbling, clutching
flung away, sudden cool breeze
passion conceived in loneliness, born of youth

deep thrusts again and again
forms slide violently
two grappling animals gasp
taste of sweat, tension pounding
smooth flesh tingling, tight, imprisoned
stretching, cracking
exploding, exploding
more more more

peace, quiet rest
light sweat on her lips
Good night.

Beautifully Spent
I lay my head between my lover's breasts
and listen to the fragile pause
in the rhythm of her heart

in this desire for pleasure
in this solace from solitude
in this unfathomable unity of lovers

a life is conceived

to bring upon the world
its strength
         or weakness

its honor
        or shame
its beauty
        or horror

then to seeks its own desire, solace, unity
        with another transient spirit
and beget another

in this manner
        is the world perpetuated
in this manner
        the most base, yet noblest of desires
        brings forth the most base and noblest of beasts

Thus the hopes and dreams and dreams of the parents
are brought forth in the reality of their children
whose own desires
will bring forth the next generation

We are but the remnants of tattered dreams
the bittersweet, brutal reality
of the past.

When I die
It will be in a small restaurant such as this
With an empty demi of wine before me
And a half empty glass
An after-dinner coffee awaiting my lips.
And as the wine lulls me into sleep
I'll look across the table to the brown-eyed lass
(my granddaughter no doubt)
With your sparkling teeth
Glowing pink smile
And deep Chinese eyes
And breathe my last.

Skimming over the water
through forests of evergreen and gentle life
to the top of the island peak
relief for the soul, hope for the man
Puget Sound and islands stretched out below

Over there snow-capped Olympics
in a beauty conceivable only
      in the mind of God
northward over water rich in blue
to Canada's misty mountains
Vancouver's misty skyline
east the Cascades' snowy splendor
west a mountain silhouette
sun setting beyond Victoria
      Empress of the Strait

Darkness from the coming night
cool, magical
losing itself in your eyes of starlight
lips as red as the western horizon
heart beating gentle as waves from the sea
touch as light as the whisper of the wind
memories

Wind and rain
Lightning, thunder
From the black eons of time
Into the sky-blue eyes of a pretty woman
Becoming the deep sea blue
Eyes of God.
Infinity
Myriads of whitecaps, rainbows following
The slap of waves against a ship
The laughter of an infant
The last breath of an old man
To become the desire of new lovers
Conception
Birth

When in the darkest hours the moonlight
Lies across your silken face
Ominously shining a pale bone-white
I shudder
And hold you tight.

the turquoise night
drifts into your eyes
of obsidian

shallow dreams
linger

dawn reveals
the remnants of the night

we lay on an edge of dust
in streets of twilight
caught in a hoary mist
suspended between heaven
and hell

Were you to leave
The wind would be gone from my sails
I would be adrift
Beneath the sun's withering rays
On empty seas

The Trap

Drowning in confusion and whiskey
your love
reaches no hearts
only lovers.

Touch my hand.
Let me caress your eyes with mine.
Touch your lips to mine.
As gently as thought turns to memory
smile and warm this heart
with tenderness and laughter.
Cry.
My shoulder needs your tears
as your lonely soul needs it.

Lovers of life
terrified of the world
we shrink into ourselves
tormented for our cowardice by fear.

Let me hold you
touch you
kiss you
caress you.

I feel the soft moisture of your lips
my hands on your back
holding you closer I feel
the softness of your breasts.
We kiss still as our lips part
tongues lightly searching.
My hands drop lower
lower.
Heartbeats race.

You start to writhe
moan.
Your tender hands
are everywhere.
I have fallen into the trap.

Eyes of eternal darkness shining through the night
Shining white teeth flashing
Firm, hard body ripping men like a knife
You're the wicked animal that has destroyed my life,

My soul.

Now you stand between me and my home,
A memory under which to suffer in shame,
Slipping into my mind from which is no escape.

My lips burn with sparks of hell,
Left there from a love well worn
          By many a drunken sailor.
Leave me with a lie.
Leave me with filth in my mind that can
          Never be cleansed.

Touching

He began by lightly kissing her eyes
then in a slow, deliberate process
worked
     down
         the length
            of her body
until by the time he had passed the knees
not an inch remained that had not been covered
with a deep, probing kiss
but when most lovers would have stopped
at the ankles
he lovingly took each toe into his mouth
caressing it with his tongue
lightly teasing it with his teeth
massaging it with warm, moist lips
sending ten unnerving shudders
flashing through her spine
to release in quivering flesh
     and arching back   .
So they continued throughout the night until,
exhausted, drifting into euphoria,
they fell asleep in each other's warm embrace.

In the soft rays of dawn she awoke alone
again.
Resigning herself to fate,
and another pointless one-night stand
she walked into the kitchen to start the day.
Coffee in hand, engrossed in the paper,
she heard the door softly close behind her.
She turned to find him there, rose in hand.

Wrapping her arms about his neck,
she wept.

As they stood embracing,
he discovered
the most sensitive parts of a person
are those that a lover
touches the least.

The Twilight of the Gods

When the dawn breaks against the velvet night
Leaving your warm embrace
I rise enchanted by the surreal light.

Forgive me
I am but a man
Tempted by beauty
Weak
By nature

"Have you?" she will ask, her eyes all the time demanding
lies

Now the few remaining stars
Disappear like the deities of the past
To leave a man with but a single god
To be betrayed with a purchased kiss
Purchased with the coins of silver in your eyes.

"Have you?" she will ask, her eyes all the time demanding
lies

How can I tell her of the treason hidden in this darkest of
souls?
That a man creates his own hell,
And this is mine: after the tears have flown and all is
forgiven,
Forever hence to speak the truth
Only to perceive a lingering doubt as she struggles to
believe.

"Have you?" she will ask, her eyes all the time demanding
lies

Yesterday
      we were a dream to be achieved
Today
      we are a stark reality
Tomorrow
      a distant memory of veiled Camelot

Night
running through the forests
cascading through the streets
        brings a
whisper of
        silences past and
time lost to eternity
flowing into the bays
        rising
ripping away
        the mask of day
leaving those remnants
        which are stars
each the sum of
millions of fireballs
the size of our world

in some far distant era
our kind will fade
into the limitless cosmos
wars will pass like wildfires
empires shall rise and fall
our troubles, travails, and glories
will all come to naught

you and I will close our eyes
and rest for all eternity
we will have had each other
but for only a spark
in the conflagration of the ages
all of these I would gladly trade
for a moment more with you

Life brief as a dream
Into which we slowly fade
And from which we oft times
Quietly awake

(Brilliance of color and senses reeling
Swirling in a vast panorama
Dazzles the mind

Passion tender as a lover's voice
In the misty sunrise
Splashing golden warmth upon the sheets

Cold and sharp as the blade
Of a vengeful broken heart)

Wrap your arms around my neck, my love
whisper into my ear
all those sultry things
I wish to hear.

Softly call my name in your sleep.
Feel my presence wrap you in its solace
caressing you in the chill night
possessing you with incredible delight.

Press your head against my chest, love.
Put your arms around me
as we dance slowly across the floor
passing time until I leave.

As a soul between traumas
The stereo has stopped.
Thoughts pass silently through my mind.
Portraits of beautiful women on the wall
Silent, intriguing
Delicate, superstitious
The furnace pops lightly.
The pen screams as it scratches the page.
Silence surrounds me
As the sea surrounds a drowning man
Filling his ears with the screams of the infinite.
Wind blows through the chimney.
I sleep alone.

Sorrow's night
fills us with bitter tears
and leaves us with spirits of stone
it hides among the shadows as the nameless fear
and reminds us we are most definitely alone

We lack the courage to face the fight
but as darkness ends in bloody dawn
our weary eyes strain for the faintest light
and somehow we find the strength to press on

The cold night wind
brushes against the windows
whispering plaintively.

The room is chill and nearly silent
but for the slight hum of the refrigerator.

a vague voice from the next room
a key rattles in the far hallway

somehow I feel at home

Have you not noticed in the spectral dawn
a bitter honesty
stealing the heart of the night
moving to compassion
the languor of the day?

My companions are strangers
My destination unknown
My purpose hazy
My past a mystery

My home far away
How did I come to be here?
I can give only answers
Nothing else

A mellow drunken numbness
Flows through my body
My soul quiets
My eyes hang heavy
Music from the stereo dampens
I wait
I rest
I sleep

I wish I could slip away into your eyes again
Become lost in the sparkle of passion released
        In the starlit Denver night
And reborn in the rising sun
As its soft bright rays filter through the
        clear Colorado sky
Through wispy curtains by my nightstand

Take me back to those eyes
        I can never have again

When the tide of night envelops Sharm El Sheikh
the desert wind blows like a warm current
carrying the laughter and music downstream
where it mingles with the talk of
wars and terrorists
   murder and politics
     the chaotic world beyond the Sinai
while the shadow of Moses looks down
on Germans
   and French
    and Swedes
      and Americans
       and Egyptians
relaxing in their world beyond the world

and I swear always to love the hometown girl
when the girl I'm with walks away
   apologizing for having to rise early
and I walk into the eyes of the waitress
   as into the desert night

Eyes made of the Egyptian night
Sparkling like an oasis pool
Skin the color of the endless sand
Beauty of forgotten goddesses lives on

headlights
glowing bigger
brighter
they come out of the mists of time
and pass beyond my vision
blinding my mind and senses
for an instant they are clear
and reach their apex
a brief hint of fog between us
disappearing
gone
more come and go
in groups or singly
an incessant line
yet broken
lives behind those lights
full of pleasure, pain, tragedy
dying, exuberant with life
in from the mists of time they pass me
I know them all too briefly
or not at all
the fog remains

they sit at their tables and stare
eyes cool, observant, bored
shells of humanity with countless faces
the same stale soul
laughter and loving have died
smoke, music, and hopeless dreams
fill the air
desire, fear, loneliness without end
winning is for others
isolation is for the damned

heat lightning
flame without warmth
heating the meaningless words
of men without souls
the flame
the dull, distant flash
vague and without beauty
lighting the darkening world
hiding the stars
then vanishing
into a sky without hope

On the walk to my apartment
Stars smile on me with eternal light
glimmers of hope
a hacking cough rips my lungs
the curse of smoky barrooms
and an empty life
I won't bitch. I won't complain.
Whimpering is for the doomed.
The living press on.

Beneath the persistent fog
the subtle rain eases
the pain of the chill
parking lot its asphalt
beaten hard by the blustery
storms of the night
rushing in from the mad sea
as gray dawn lingers
waiting for the reticent sun
we emerge from the bygone
dreams and fears of youth
as a man too long under water
breaks the surface gasping

now we must clutch
onto shards of reality
as a drowning man
clutches onto wayward driftwood
praying that he does not
drown in that which
rules his life
all the time waiting
for sight of land

Among drifting guests and pointless chatter
I sat brooding on days to come
wrapped in twilight's slanting rays
at a party under a mango tree

then a sudden movement caught my eye
as a fragrance from the past drifted on air
and a familiar silhouette hovered beyond the gate

startled I noticed her

drifting silently into the tattered shade
for a heartbeat lingering there
with haunting smile and dark eyes
before vanishing in the dusty breeze

slowly shattered memories made their way
back through the remnants of the sun
to disappear among the lengthening shadows

The storm comes slowly
      building its madness
      until in a gentle, almost subtle rain
      or frenzy of thunder and dazzling light
It releases its power
its creation
flowing through my mind
and spirit
and onto the page.

then spent
as a lover
I drift into a relaxing smile
drift into a reverie of the soul
wondering where you are.

Sunlight reflecting off distant peaks
stings the eyes as cold, crisp silence
chills the soul with church-like peace
blankets the spirit with warm serenity

tiny cars slowly wind up the gray valley
far below in the temporal world

behold the sun
slipping beneath its crimson blankets
as he shakes off their red dust
which settles like the ash
of a thousand broken hearts

there he sleeps
below the horizon
between me and my love

Might Have Been...

though we never kissed
nor even touched
though it has been many lovers since

still
her face surfaces in the sea of dreams

still
her delicate nose and tender smile
do not brush against my ear

still
the rolling lilt of her voice
does not whisper its love songs
into the hollows of my soul

The cold night wind brushes against the windows
whispering plaintively

the room is chill and nearly silent
but for the slight hum of the refrigerator

a vague voice from the next room
a key rattles in the far hallway

somehow I feel at home

The cool winds of Autumn
bring a dusting of leaves
and barren trees
to the endless rows
of those
who have faded into the past.

a life is only an epitaph
written as lived

John
beloved husband and father

Margaret
her life was a beacon on a troubled sea

Thomas
as long as we live, he lives among us still

but
so many names
and only dates.

In the other room
Madness awaits.
He peeks around the corner
my heart races; nerves
tighten as a bow string
Or is it finally sanity?

There is madness in silence
Rooted in the fears of the heart

Terrors of solitude

he sits alone
scotch in one hand
cigarette in the other
and waits
eyeing the crowd
watching the dance floor
picking out the honies
and waits
no movement escapes
his eye
he watches every girl
as she walks past
watches who she walks in with
watches who she walks out with
The staff all know him.

the night caressed the land
      like a black silk shift
smooth
noiseless
cool and soft to the touch
as I settled between the bedsheets
      head beneath the window
I felt the night seep in
      running across my face
      in a cold current
bringing memories of moonlight
      long ago
      filtering through my curtains
      sparkling in your dark eyes
      like dreams

"What, am I like any other woman?" she asked.
His own lips broke barely into a smile as if to say
yes.

     Like the tramps and the virgins
     Like the bar-sweepings and the would-be saints
     Like the wives and divorcees

And at night
though she rustles the sheets beside him
wrapping her warm arms around his chest
                  he sleeps alone

He can give you a home and a family.
He will always be there when you need him.
He will always kiss you when he comes home.
But
I can make you claw the headboard in ecstasy,
And give you a dream to keep you warm
In your old, old age.

her soft voice no longer echoes into my ear
her soft hair no longer brushes against my cheek
her soft eyes no longer sparkle in the silken night
but still her face surfaces in the sea of dreams

cigar smoke swirls like vanishing dreams
dancing a slow, vaporous waltz
i have created a phantom of ash
lasting only a few fragile heartbeats
riding the unperceived currents of air
cavorting like silent stallions through my home
nicotine caresses my lungs
bringing pseudopeace to a troubled mind

many analogies can be made
with the transient whimsical forms
arising serenely above my head
the fickle convoluted desires that are humanity
the passage of time and the vain
        search for immortality
but in their essence what are all of these
only the twistings of the mind
riding the demands of the times
like smoke on currents of air

An Evening Stroll through Chinatown and North Beach,
San Francisco, 1993

I arrived
sun low, not yet setting
must have been around 8:00

Split a table at a crowded Chinese
restaurant with a radio d.j.
Incredible food.
We talked long,
left when the light was dim,
said good-bye.
I went up a block,
stopped by a microbrewery
for a beer,
asked directions to a tobacco shop.

On the way for cigars
a Hindi girl leaning in a doorway
asks to read my palm
I hesitate
"You have great problems. I can tell.
Come back."
I go on, pick up the cigars, and return.
She leads me to a spacious upstairs room
with a shag rug,
ivory and leather couch around the walls.
A middle-aged man and a little girl watch TV
"I have a customer. Please leave."
The man departs, the child stays and
turns the sound off, leaving a spent, ghostly image.
The girl reads my palm and I leave,
her words lingering in my mind,
like warm, stagnant air.

Outside an aged Chinese woman sells
pornography on the street.

I drop by an upper class Italian club.
On the other side of the bar
a man with strong arms and soft hands
discusses hot tubs
with a healthy Italian girl.
Now and then she glances at me,
knowing,
questioning.

A few steps down the street,
in a dingy corner saloon,
the bass violin player
in a three piece band
belts out R&B based rock
and a "little red rooster" that'll
steal your soul.

Down the street a neon sign flashes:
NUDE
NUDE
NUDE
LIVE GIRLS
while underneath a woman in black and pink
with pseudo-ebony eyes
beckons.
Just another siren of the nuclear age.

Talk in the bars centers on Koresh
and the children dying at Waco.
Tear gas?
Suicide?

Deep in the red and green neon
of Chinatown German tourists
question their maps while
a wino screams out an obscene
plea for forgiveness to a neon god
as he roots through the trash
while papers and whispers
blow down the alleyways.

The stripper in one joint was from Seattle,
had moved to Frisco with her roommate
who settled here.
Only started two weeks ago.
Sweet girl
($40 for drinks and conversation)
She mounts the stage proudly
for teachers and salesmen
as the homeless beg for change
on every street corner
(one had his sleeping bag stolen
the other homeless call him stupid).

Tomorrow's front page is already out:
Montana says no to 49er's.
Beneath is the story of Koresh
and the 86 who died in the blaze.

I enter a bar
next to the psychic's place,
where a man loudly berates the government
to a colleague with alarming clarity
and the rotten smell
of truth gone bad.

The psychic's words still linger:
"You have many problems.

You are very confused.
You love doing good for others,
but you get none in return.
You will live a long life.
You will have many sorrows
and many joys.
I will pray for you if you want.
Do you want me to pray for you?"

"Yes."

"Many sorrows. Many joys.
I will light a candle for you.
I will light nine candles for you.
Do you want me to light nine candles for you?"

"Yes."

"Many sorrows. Many joys.
Each drop of wax that drops or runs
down the side of each candle
will bring a new joy,
will be a sorrow relieved.
Do you want me to light nine candles for you?"

"Yes."

"Because the candles come all the way
from Jerusalem
they are $20 each.
Do you want me to light the candles for you?"

"I'll pass.
Leave them for someone who needs them more."
I pay her twenty and leave.

The psychic comes in and passes,
looking at everyone but me.
She goes upstairs
comes back in ten minutes,
looking at everyone but me,
passing me by.
She's a beautiful, blind ghost in another world.

Talk in the bar centers on Koresh
and the ghoulish press.
I meet Joe there.
He talks about the police in Argentina.
"Make evidence gained by torture
inadmissible in court
and they'll stop torturing.
That's what scares me about proposition 18,
it makes everything admissible."
Joe continues.
He had been a victim of torture.
He says.
He says he knows
what he's talking about.
His conversation turns
to how the best clams are
from El Salvador.
They're famous, world-famous,
he says.

Outside
A madman screams obscenities
at a lamp post
while the bartenders talk
about candy bars.

The stripper's conversation was sweet
until I ran out of money.

I walk outside,
light up a cigar,
and drift away.

Sign in the bar says,
"Everyone here brings joy
Some by entering
Some by leaving."

Death of a Poet

it comes
like the...stinking dawn
bright, golden, and slowly
creeping like a cancer
a clarity of mind, thought, and emotion
gone are the nights when the stars
hung like burning jewels
in a smoke-ridden void
gone is the memory
of the taste of a woman's dew
as the door clicks solemnly after her
gone is the sweet remorse
of a life without purpose
except to pour onto paper
all that is felt, sensed, and devoured
replaced with a damnable clarity
a perception keen as a blade
that gives the world the taste of cold steel
and the feel of a chilling dawn

Perdition's Children

we have loved and lost and loved again
the nights are not so bitter
the days are not so dark

we are perdition's children
in pursuit of a temporal grail

cancers arise from our lungs
and tinge yellow once sacred skies

chemicals flow through our veins
and liquefy our immaculate thoughts

sacred waters convey our filth

come, let us escape this, our own creation
leave our fluorescent brood to neon wolves

come, let us shatter the boundaries of art
then extol our icons of junk

we worship the meaningless and call it holy
we crave full bellies and bloated egos

discard your worn lover and join us now

carpe carpe carpe diem we sing

we grieve not and escape into hollow laughter

there is no sorrow to which the mind
        cannot be calloused

no pain from which we cannot escape

into a drug

forget your future and join us
in abandonment to sweet sensual perdition

we have lost and loved and lost again
the days are so bitter
the nights are so dark

tragicomedy
of midnight bars
dance floor lights twinkle
pseudostars
for pseudolovers
beneath the rhythm
of the barroom haze

subtle maddening differences
of forlorn eyes
broken by tedium
of distilled hopes
cigarette smoke
a lonely current
in the sea of night
bourbon laughter echoes
through the hollows of time

laughter of friends
and giggles of lovers
break the vacant stares
of would-be Romeos
for the night

empty beds
of ruffled sheets

the next bar
dreams become reality
maybe the next bar

Gentle buzz. Very gentle buzz.

starry night
the placid heavens belie
the turmoil of the cosmos
the constellations swirl slowly
in perpetual dance
the lights of the city
blind men
to the lessons of the past

dreams are the philosophies of the night
we read their symbols
to delve into their essence and discover
what secrets lie chained within our souls
then at the end of a long night's journey
we open our eyes
to sleep a better dream

When the spirit of the night has sung its last song
then will I close my eyes in sweet sleep
to await the bright sunshine

Sweet sleep
how I wait for you at times
to bring rest to these weary bones.
But still the night is young
And the bands still play lively tunes
While the strong drink has not yet dulled my senses
Nor put an end to my longing for the night.

There will be time for rest when the cool dawn comes
revealing all in its bright omniscient light
burning away the blackness surrounding this mysterious
world
while I rest from my wanderings
to arise late with a groggy head and start anew

I love the night as a favorite lover.
even as I sleep will I still feel its cool embrace
listening to its gentle murmurings
my ear feels the pulse of its heart
as I lean my head on its breast.
How eagerly I await the coming night.
Should the day never end,
I would fade away of despair.

'Tis only the promise of another beloved night
that quickens my heart and pace
brings youth to my steps and vigor to my love
as the years pass like eternity
to the time I can rest forever.

The Dead Poet Awaits Resurrection

these are the confines of my coffin
that looking at a leaf
      I see only a leaf
that feeling the wind on my face
      I feel only the wind
that walking into the sun
      I feel only warmth
and remembering you
      I remember only one among many

where are the days
      when your voice flowed and sparkled
      like liquid sunlight across snow-capped mountains?
where are the nights
      when the stars lay strewn across the heavens
      like kisses across your dark skin?
where are the mornings
      when warm embraces mingled with the
      cold air of cheap hotels
      like coffee with cream?

the gentleness that once wrapped itself around you
now has a cold, sharp edge
its arms are tough and sinewy
its chest is scarred from battles for its soul

the roads that separate us
are long and twisting under
vague memories
dissipating like distant storms

dawn is rising somewhere
each moment is a new beginning
i tell myself

but i weary of dawn
the day i left
i drove off
as the sun broke the horizon
now i cannot find the dawn

the bow of the ship
divides the ocean
like the blade
of a hundred-foot knife
neatly slicing
the union
of sea and sky

beyond the lingering horizon
lurks land
beyond the veil of light
hide the stars
glimmering
like the myriad drops of sun
breaking against the waves and swells
leading us on
to a distant shore

Stretching out through the vastness of time
I am the whole of all I have done
or been
the loathsome and the beautiful
the wretched and the wonderful
the ugly and the innocent
these have I looked upon
and expect yet again
as my life slowly winds its way
through the misty forest of the future
to its end

I dedicate this book, once again, to my wife,
Francene Kilgore Slattery,
My best and truest friend and the embodiment of love.

August 8, 2020

Nocturne
Poems of Love, Distance, and the Night,
a callous and disinterested lover
first print edition
August 8, 2020

Acknowledgements

"An Unfamiliar Sensuality" published in Nefarious Ballerina in January 2010.

"The Twilight of the Gods", "The Trap", and "Touching" published in Apollo's Lyre in February 2010.

"The Women of Cairo":   Unfortunately, at the moment I do not have a record of where this poem was first published. As best I recall, it was published sometime between 1988 and 1991. I found, accidentally, the poem cited in the blog Rays and Shadows around fifteen years after it was first published. I have always felt it a great honor to have a work quoted years after it was published. That means it, and I, made an impact on someone. This link tells the serendipitous story of the poem.   Thank you, Khaled of Cairo, Egypt, for remembering me.

Following are several poems that I have in my records on hands only as "published". I cannot recall exactly where and when each was published originally, but they were all published in the early nineties. Several are about Egypt, where I was stationed at the US embassy in Cairo from August to September of 1989. Some were written from 1986-1988 when I lived in Oak Harbor on Whidbey Island in Puget Sound northwest of Seattle: "Apology", "Drifting", "Empty", "En Passant" (*En Passant* is a move in chess, wherein a pawn takes another pawn), "Gap", "Insomnia", "Love's First Light", "Sharm El Sheikh", "Still", "Taste", and "Lovers' Dreams".

"The Desert Wind" was published in Potpourri, March, 1993.

Here is a partial list of publication credits dating from December, 1996 that shows where many of these were first published, though I cannot match publisher with poem at this time: *Green's Magazine*, Autumn, 1989; *Doors Into and Out of Dorset*, January, 1990; *Green's Magazine*, Spring, 1990; *Bitterroot*, Summer, 1990; *Green's Magazine*, Autumn, 1990; *Orphic Lute*, Summer, 1991; *Green's Magazine*, Winter, 1991; *Sassafras Tea* (honorable mention, Third Winter Annual Poetry Competition, 1991; and *Metro Singles Lifestyles*, approximately 10 poems, various dates.

Please forgive any errors or omissions. My records are not what they should be.

About the Author

Phil Slattery is a native of Kentucky, but now resides in New Mexico. He received a B.A. from Eastern Kentucky University in 1980. He has traveled widely in the US and abroad during his university studies and while in the US Navy. He started out writing poetry from 1985 to 1995. Currently, he writes mostly horror and dark fiction, but he dabbles in other literary forms and genres as well. Many of his works are rooted in his experiences while traveling. His fiction has been published in *Futures Mysterious Anthology Magazine, Ascent Aspirations, Medicinal Purposes Literary Review, Dream Fantasy International, Wilmington Blues, Möbius, Spoiled Ink, Midnight Times, Six Sentences, Sorcerous Signals, Every Day Fiction, Flash Fiction World, Through the Gaps, Fiction on the Web*, and *Creepy Campfire Quarterly.* On Thanksgiving Day, 2016, he published a novelette (*Click*) and two collections of short stories (*A Tale of Hell and Other Works of Horror* and *The Scent and Other Stories*) on Amazon Kindle, followed by *Alien Embrace* and *Diabolical: Three Tales of Jack Thurston and Revenge* in 2017. More on his writing can be found at https://philslattery.wordpress.com and at amazon.com/author/philslattery. His twitter handle is @philslattery201. He can be found on other social media as well.

Made in the USA
Monee, IL
25 August 2020